Fairytale fancy dress

Fairytale fancy dress

Anke Vogt

D-Books International-Hartlebury

Bell-House productions
Copyright ©1988 by D-Books International Ltd. Kiddermaster, UK.
Translation: The Old Rectory.

ISBN 1-870594-01-0

English Edition distributed by **Ruskin Book services Ltd.**
Unit 306
Hartlebury Trading Estate
Hartlebury
Worcs. DY10 4JB, United Kingdom
Telephone (0299) 251505
Telex 339288 VR1 NTL
Fax (0299) 251576

Printed in Italy by New-Interlitho SpA

Contents

Foreword

Many fairytales begin 'Once upon a time...' The more contact children have with fairytales and stories, the more the world of their imagination can expand.

Children love to pretend to be characters from their dreams. This is even more fun if they can dress up. What child would not enjoy being the Little Mermaid, Rumplestilskin, the Sorcerer's Apprentice or Ali Baba?

This book gives advice for anyone who would like to bring these fairytale characters to life, together with children.

Fairytale Fancy Dress contains eleven patterns for making the costumes for fairytales.

The simple patterns and clear instructions ensure that your creations will allways be a success. In most cases the choice of material is not particularly important. You can achieve miracles with basic materials and even with old garments.

Not only the costumes but also the make-up to complement them, are described step by step with the use of examples.

Making the costumes and doing the make-up for children is great fun in itself.

Fairytale Fancy Dress is a must for anyone, child or adult. It should be on the shelves at school, at youth clubs, libraries, and certainly in your own home.

General guidelines

Patterns and sizes

The patterns in this book are drawn to scale. Every square on the pattern paper represents 4 x 4 cm (2 x 2"). This pattern paper is available from handicraft shops and department stores.

The eleven costumes for children aged approximately 5 to 10 are shown in small, medium and large sizes. The small size is for little ones of 5 and 6 years old, the medium for children aged 7 to 8, and the large size for older children of 9 to 10. On the work sheets all patterns for jump suits, shirts and trousers are marked with the letters S, M and L.

The tops and other jackets are drawn in a single size, as these are worn over the costumes. Where required, these patterns can be enlarged or reduced according to what is needed. It is advisable to try the pattern on the child before sewing the costume, taking special care to check the length of sleeves and trouser legs. Thus the sizes are *not* the same as those of normal children's clothes. You can make the alterations yourself by altering the side seams or lengthening or shortening the sleeves and trouser legs.

An attempt has been made to give short and clear instructions, so that making these costumes is a simple matter. The jump suits, tops and shirts are loose fitting. Ankward fastenings are replaced by elastic, Velcro, and hooks and eyes so that putting on and taking off the costume is not a problem — even for the smallest children. They will have complete freedom of movement in these party clothes.

Finishing off and fastening

The costumes are finished off with a small row of zig-zag stitching, a hem or with bias binding. The fasteners to be used include press-studs, hooks and eyes and Velcro. There is no need to use facing.

Stitching

The tops and capes are separate parts of the costume and they are reinforced by being stitched onto a layer of foam plastic. This foam plastic is about 1.5 cm ($^3/_4$") thick and is available from virtually any shop selling materials or furnishing fabrics; it is better for this purpose than the usual fibre fill. Because of its rough surface the material can easily be pulled taut and does not move about when it is sewn.

There is no need for tacking the costumes; they only need to be pinned.

Stitching may be difficult on a sewing machine, but this can be remedied in two ways:

1. Material is used on both sides of the foam plastic, though in this case you will need twice as much material;
2. You stitch a strip of tissue paper or toilet paper onto the back of the foam plastic. This can easily be removed later.

Choice of materials

Light, stretchy materials such as cotton jersey, cotton towelling, thin cotton etc. are easy to use and generally not expensive.

Tools

For doing the make-up of the appropriate faces, you will need a mirror and a good source of light. Always work in front of the mirror so that you can catch the light directly. It is useful to have a mirror on the table so that you can move about freely. A useful size for the mirror is 60 x 40 cm. (25 x 18"), though of course it is perfectly possible to use a mirror of a completely different size. An anglepose light is a very useful form of lighting.

For the make-up you will also need:
— *sponges;* for applying the coloured make-up. The sponges are round and about 3 cm. (1¼") thick, made of foam plastic with a rather greasy feel.
— *a stippling sponge:* for coarse make-up;
— *brushes:* in varying thicknesses;
— *pencil sharpener:* for soft pencils;
— *powder puff;*
— *powder brush:* for removing excess powder;
— *comb;*
— *scissors;*
— *chamois leather:* a piece of natural chamois leather, about 10 x 15 cm (4 x 7");
— *case:* a fishing tackle case is very useful for storing all this equipment.

Materials

There are two sorts of make-up: greasepaint and water-based make-up. Greasepaint is a cream which covers less thoroughly, but is easier to blend in. Powder is need to 'fix' the make-up. Water-based make-up is more resistant, but covers better and does not need to be powdered. You will need the natural basic shades of both these types. These are flesh tinted, lighter, darker, more red or more yellow, depending on the colour of the make-up. If you use water-based make-up, you will also need additional colours such as yellow, green, blue, purple etc. for applying the patterns onto the basic make-up.

In addition, you will need:
— *pencils:* soft, greasy pencils (dermatograph) so that lines can easily be smudged. These come in various colours;
— *powder:* a neutral, light, transparent powder;
— *make-up remover:* a type of vaseline for removing greasepaint. Water-based make-up can be more easily removed with soap and water;
— *soap:* for washing the hands and sponges and, if necessary, for masking the eyebrows and the hair at the temples;
— *hairslides:* slides and grips for holding the hair in place;
— *tissues* for removing the make-up and cleaning the hands.

The Little Mermaid
Material for the body and fin
any material 180 x 120 cm (90 x 60")

Material for blouse
any material 60 x 120 cm (30 x 60")

In addition
thin foam plastic
hooks and eyes
elastic
25 cm (12") Velcro
beads and sequins
elasticated shiny hair band
bias binding 300 cm (140")

◄1►
Cut the front of the bodice from the foam plastic.
◄2►
Cut out the front from the material.
◄3►
Stitch the material onto the foam plastic with a large zig-zag stitch along the edge. The edge can easily be felt and pressed flat while you are sewing.
◄4►
Stitch the pattern seams (scales) onto the front.
◄5►
Cut out the back from the material.
◄6►
From the dotted line also cut out the back from the foam plastic.
◄7►
Stitch the material onto the foam plastic in the same way as for the front.
◄8►
Stitch the pattern seams (scales and tail) onto the back.
◄9►
Stitch up the side seams.
◄10►
Finish off the bodice with bias binding round the whole costume.
◄11►
Fasten the shoulders with hooks and eyes.
◄12►
Sew or stick sequins and beads randomly over the bodice.
◄13►
Cut out the fin from the foam plastic.

◄14►
Cut out the fin from the material 2 x and cover the foam plastic with this in the same way as the bodice.
◄15►
Stitch the decorative patterns.
◄16►
Finish off the fin with bias binding or a small zig-zag stitch.
◄17►
Stitch a length of Velcro onto the bottom of the fin
◄18►
Stitch the rest of the Velcro onto the back of the bodice in such a way that the fin can be seen on the front.
◄19►
Sew some sequins or beads onto the *hair band.*
◄20►
Cut out the *blouse.*
◄21►
Fasten centre back and shoulder seams.
◄22►
Stitch a narrow strip of foam plastic onto the inside of the sleeves and hem round.
◄23►
Stitch patterns seams onto this.
◄24►
Stitch up side seams.
◄25►
Finish off neck edge with a small hem and fasten centre back with hooks and eyes.

Accessories
Suitable tights and shoes.

Make-up for the Little Mermaid

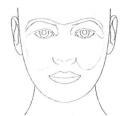 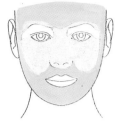  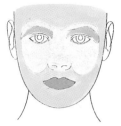

1 Use a dermatograph pencil to draw lines onto the face.

2 Colour the centre part of the face with a silvery waterbased make-up. Use light blue make-up around the silvery colour.

3 The eyelids are made up with green water-based make-up.

4 The lips are painted bright red.

Useful tip
Replace the elasticated hair band with a shawl of shiny material. The Little Mermaid could wear a number of strings of pearls.

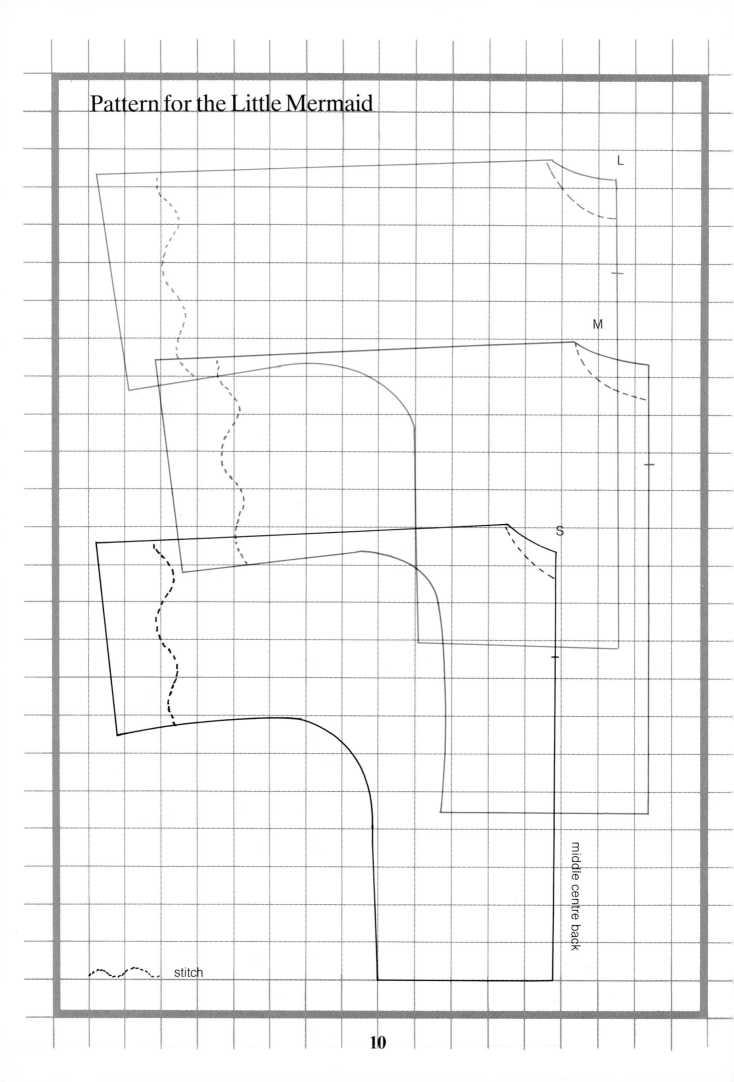

Pattern for the Little Mermaid

L

M

S

middle centre back

stitch

10

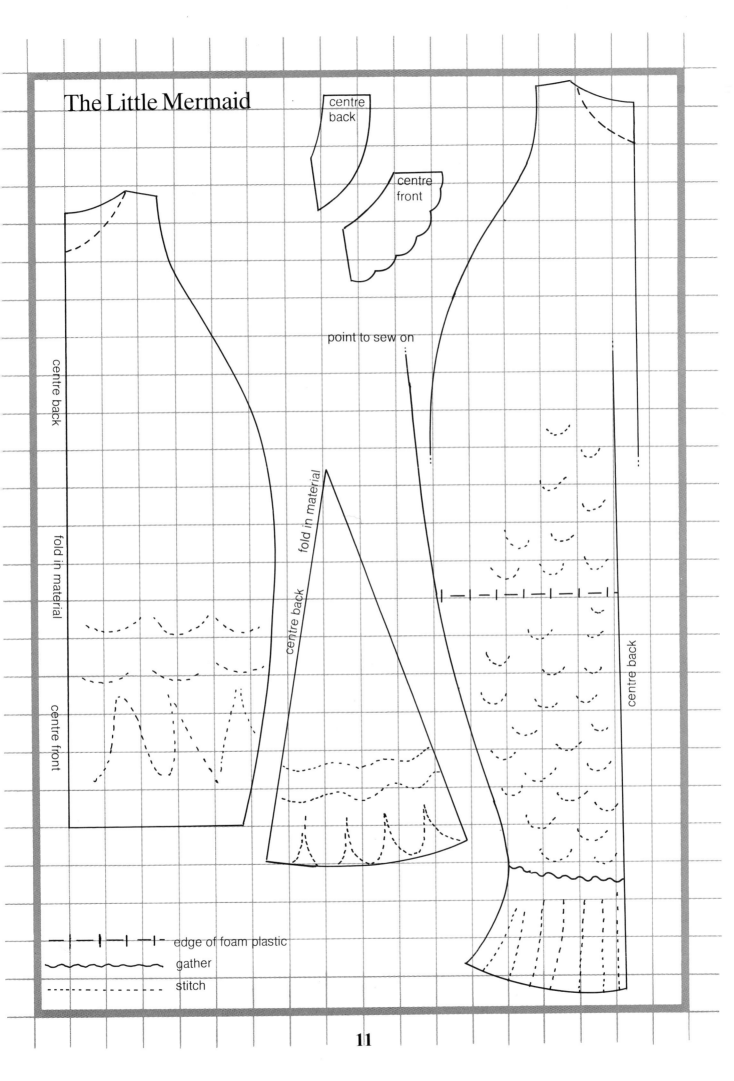

The Little Mermaid

centre back

centre front

point to sew on

centre back

fold in material

fold in material

centre back

centre back

centre front

— | — | — | — | — edge of foam plastic

gather

stitch

11

The Genie in the Bottle
Material for the main body of the bottle
any material 60 x 120 cm (30 x 60″)

Material for blouse
white cotton 50 x 120 cm (25 x 60″)

Material for hat
a remnant of white cotton from the blouse
thin card 40 x 80 cm (20 x 40″)
white or coloured gauze 50 x 120 cm (25 x 60″)

In addition
hooks and eyes or Velcro
thin foam plastic or fibre fill 60 x 120 cm (30 x 60″)

◀1▶
Cut out the blouse.
◀2▶
Sew up centre back to the indicated point. Then sew up shoulder seams.
◀3▶
Hem round the neck edge and fasten the centre back with hooks and eyes.
◀4▶
Hem the sleeves.
◀5▶
Cut out the main part of the bottle 2 x from the material.
◀6▶
Then cut out 2 x from the foam plastic or fibre fill, leaving a generous border.
◀7▶
Spread the material over the foam plastic and fold the edges back.
◀8▶
Pin down the material and stitch down, approximately 2 cm (1″) from the edge.
◀9▶
Sew shoulder seams together by hand.
◀10▶
Fit the top with the blouse underneath and join the two parts together in the side seams with hooks and eyes.
◀11▶
Cut the *collar* from the foam plastic and then from the same material as the main part of the bottle, leaving a generous border.

◀12▶
Place the material on the foam plastic, fold the edges back and stitch down the material about 2 cm (1″) from the edge.
◀13▶
Fasten the centre back with hooks and eyes.
◀14▶
Fot the *hat*, cut a circle from the card with a diameter of about 40 cm (20″).
◀15▶
Cut the circumference of a child's head from this circle.
◀16▶
Use the remaining card to make a pointed cone with a diameter slightly larger than that of the edge which you have cut.
◀17▶
Cover both parts with cotton (sew or glue).
◀18▶
Glue or staple down the sides of the pointed cone.
◀19▶
Slide the cone as far as possible into the rim and then make cuts in the bottom of the cone.
◀20▶
Fold over the flaps and glue onto the edge.
◀21▶
Fix the gauze onto the point of the cone in such a way that it can be drapped around the spirit like a cloud.
◀22▶
It is possible to sew the points of the gauze onto the sleeves of the blouse or the shoulders of the top.

Accessories
Tights and shoes.

The Genie in the Bottle Make-up

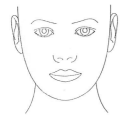 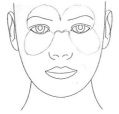  

1 White water-based make-up is applied to the face with a sponge.

2 Use a dermatograph pencil to draw the outlines around the eyes.

3 Fill the spaces inside the outline under the eyes with black water-based make-up.

4 Fill in the spaces above the eyes with green water-based make-up. The lips are made up with a wine red colour.

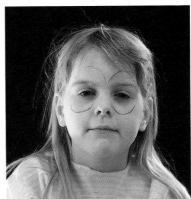

A useful tip
The hat can also be made from gold coloured card or plastic with a great deal of gauze fixed to it.

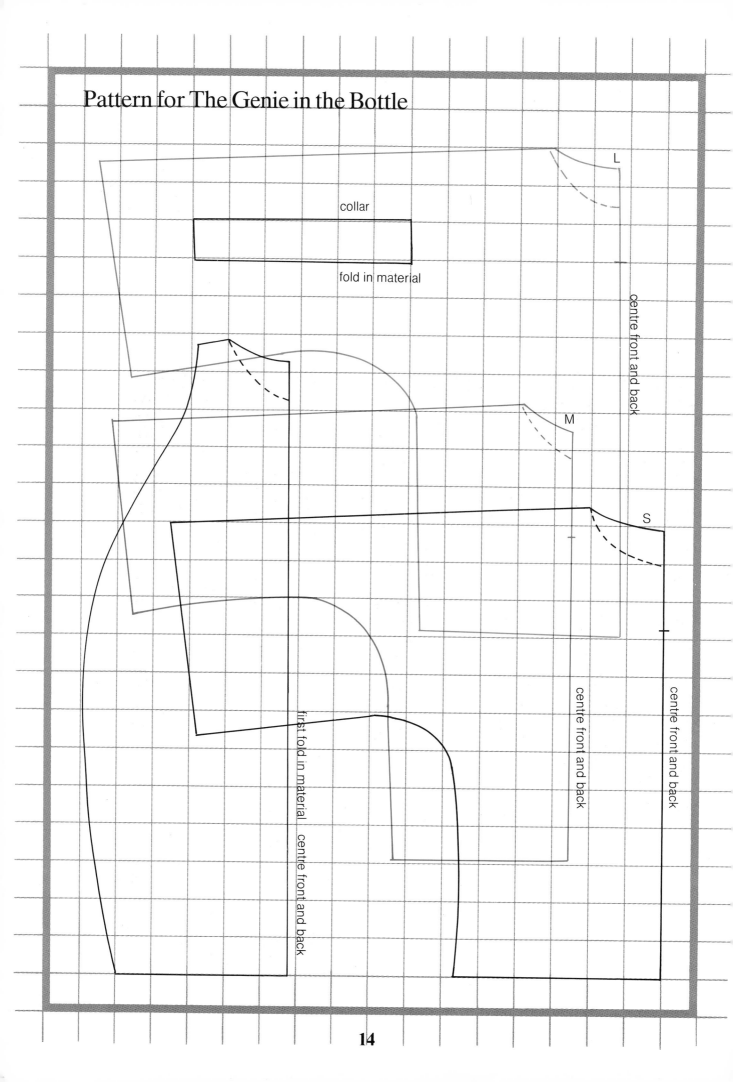

Pattern for The Genie in the Bottle

collar

fold in material

L

centre front and back

M

S

first fold in material

centre front and back

centre front and back

centre front and back

The Genie in the Bottle

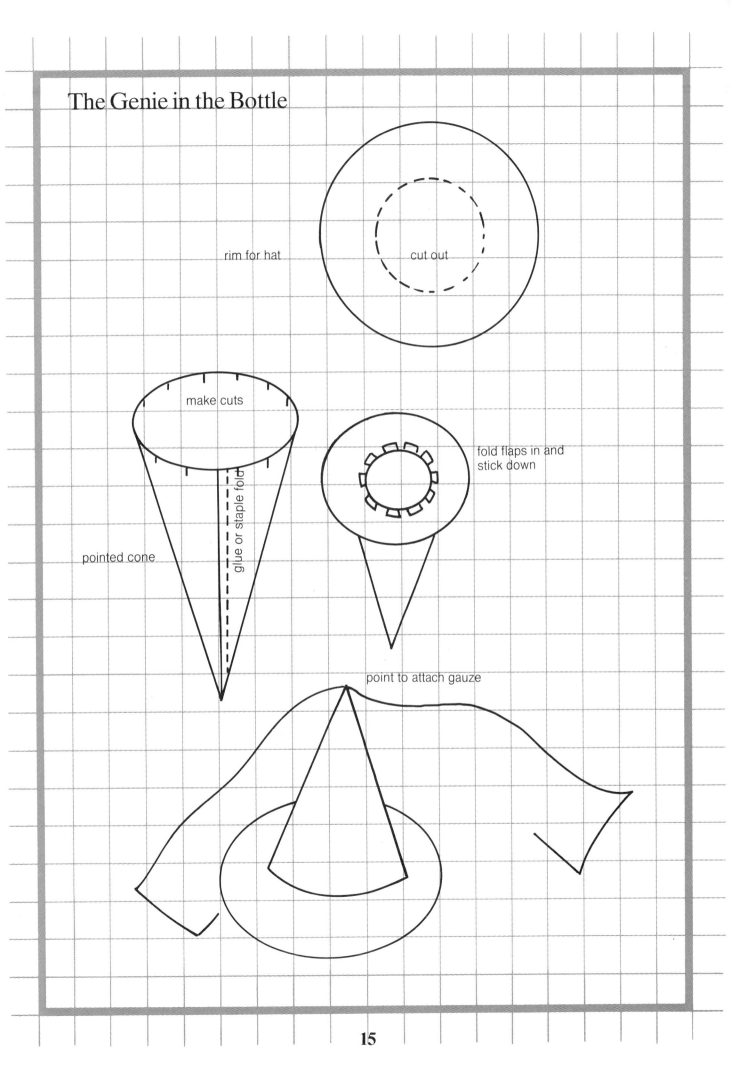

rim for hat

cut out

make cuts

glue or staple fold

pointed cone

fold flaps in and stick down

point to attach gauze

Rumpelstiltskin

Material for blouse
any material 60 x 120 cm (30 x 60″)

Material for trousers
any material 100 x 120 cm (50 x 60″)

Material for cape and collar
any material 40 x 120 cm (20 x 60″)

In addition
2 hanks of gold thread for beard
elastic
hooks and eyes

◄1►
Cut out the blouse.
◄2►
Sew centre back up to the indicated point.
◄3►
Sew shoulder and side seams.
◄4►
Cut out the bottom unevenly and zig-zag round the edges.
◄5►
Finish off neck edge and sleeves with hem.
◄6►
Fasten centre back with hooks and eyes.
◄7►
Cut out the *trousers*.
◄8►
Sew up centre back, centre front and outside leg seams.
◄9►
Cut out appliqué pattern 2 x.
◄10►
Sew pattern onto the bottom of the trouser legs in such a way that the centre of the pattern lies on the outside leg seam.
◄11►
Zig-zag the pattern on the material with a small zig-zag stitch.
◄12►
Sew up inside leg seams.
◄13►
Pass elastic through bottom of trouser legs and waist.

◄14►
Cut out the *collar*.
◄15►
Cut out the *hood* twice.
◄16►
Fasten the two pieces of the hood together.
◄17►
Place the two parts right side together. Sew the two pieces together, except for the bottom.
◄18►
Hem centre front of the collar.
◄19►
Lay hood on right side of collar. Sew up the inside by hand.
◄20►
The beard:
Sew the thread in lenghts of about 20 cm (10″) onto a thin strip of cotton about 25 cm (12″) long.
◄21►
Cut off the bottom of the thread evenly.
◄22►
Sew elastic onto the ends of the strip of cotton so that the beard fastens round the head by the ears.

Accessories
shoes or boots
belt
pin or ribbon to fasten hood/collar.

Rumpelstiltskin make-up

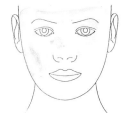 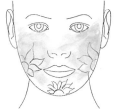 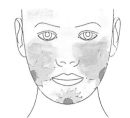 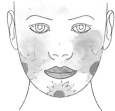

1 Apply a light natural water-based make-up to the face with a sponge.

2 Use water-based make-up to apply a red blush to both cheeks.

3 Outline the eyebrows with light brown water-based make-up.

4 The lips are made up the same colour as the dress.

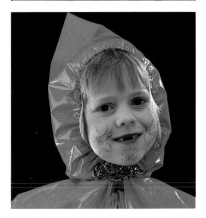

A useful tip
Gold nail varnish and a belt of gold leather or gold material enhance the overall effect.

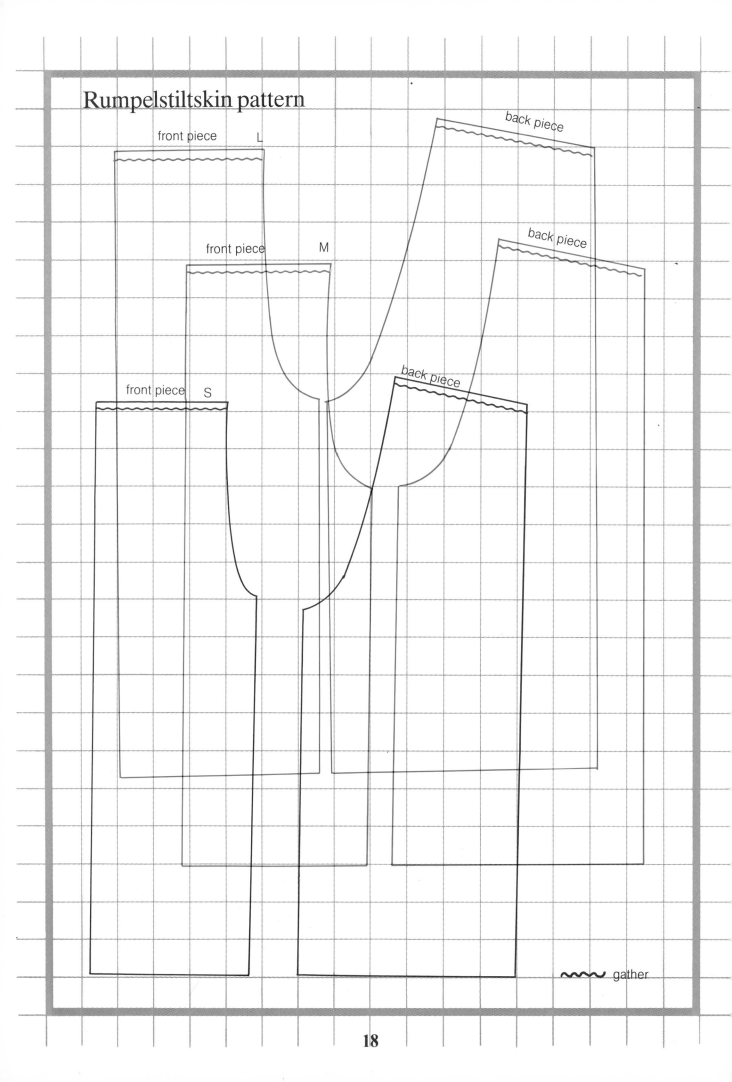

Rumpelstiltskin pattern

front piece L

back piece

front piece M

back piece

front piece S

back piece

〜〜〜 gather

18

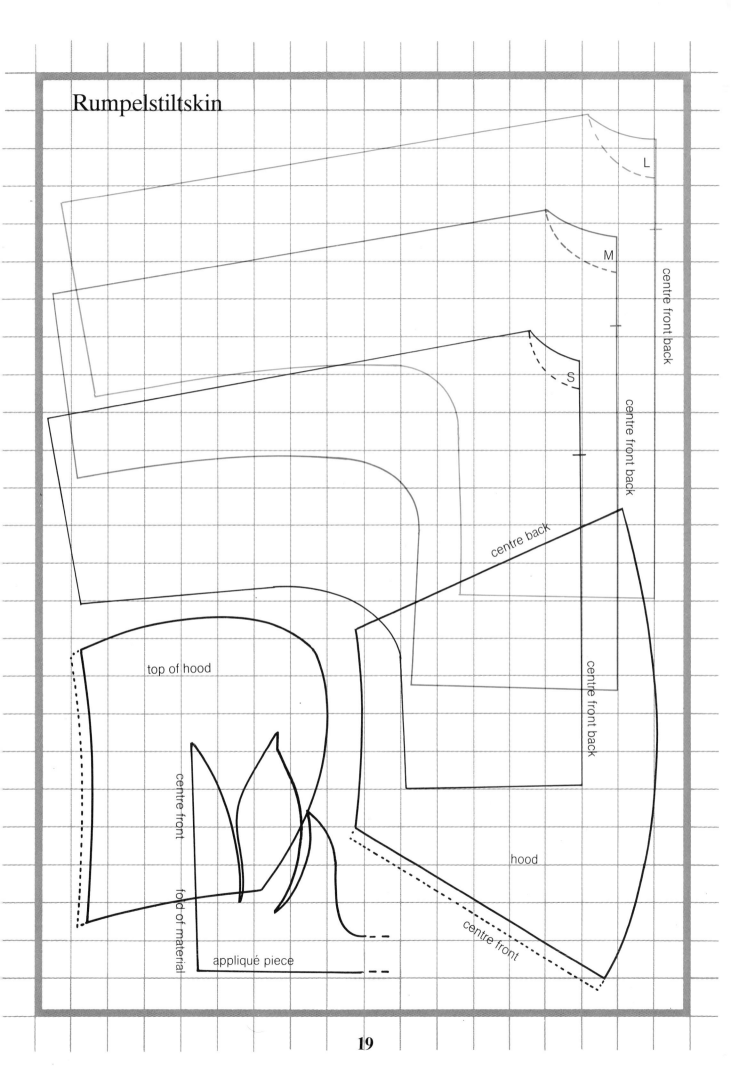

Rumpelstiltskin

L

M

S

centre front back

centre front back

centre front back

centre front back

centre back

top of hood

centre front

fold of material

appliqué piece

hood

centre front

19

The Princess and the Frog
Material for the dress
any material, 120 x 120 cm (60 x 60")

Material for pattern and webbed feet
green material 60 x 60 cm (30 x 30")

In addition
thin foam plastic or fibre fill, 30 x 120 cm (15 x 60")
gold coloured card
5 green beads
1 sheet of green felt card
1 transparent plastic folder, A4 size
elastic
hooks and eyes

◄1►
Cut out the *dress.*
◄2►
Sew up centre back to indicated place.
◄3►
Sew up shoulder and side seams.
◄4►
Place a strip of foam plastic or fibre fill along the bottom of the inside of the dress.
◄5►
Make a small hem.
◄6►
Pin material down on the foam plastic/fibre fill.
◄7►
Draw the reeds onto the front with a pencil.
◄8►
Stitch along the outline.
◄9►
Cut out a number of patterns from the green materiaal.
◄10►
Stitch these onto the dress randomly with a small zig-zag stitch.
◄11►
Thread elastic through neck edge and sleeves.
◄12►
For the mask, cut an oval shape from the felt card, 10 cm (5") wider than the child's face on either side.
◄13►
Cut out a long triangle where the mouth should be.
◄14►
Reinforce the back with an extra strip of card and fasten elastic to this.

◄15►
Cut two circles with a diameter of about 10 cm (5") from the plastic.
◄16►
These are glued onto the back of the mouth in such a way that a large part of the cheeks sticks up above the mouth.
◄17►
Cut out the *webbed feet* 2 x from the foam plastic and 2 from the green material with a wide margin. Place the material on the foam plastic and smooth out.
◄18►
Stitch the material onto the edge of the foam plastic with a small zig-zag stitch. It is easy to feel the edge while you are sewing and fold it flat.
◄19►
Stitch seams to form the pattern.
◄20►
Attach the webbed feet above the shoes with a piece of elastic.

Accessories
lace gloves
shoes
green tights

Tip
Cut a crown from gold paper and fix thin elastic onto the sides.

Make-up for the Princess and the Frog

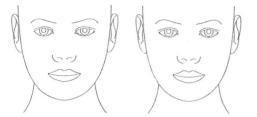 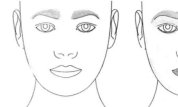 

1 Apply a light natural coloured make-up thinly and evenly to the face.

2 Apply a bluish-green water-based make-up unevenly to the face.

3 Use a thin brush to apply dark green water-based make-up to the eyebrows.

4 Use a brush to apply a silvery water-based make-up to the eyelids. The lips are coloured bright red.

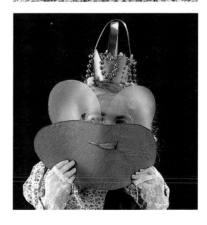

Useful tips
Draw a crown onto gold coloured card and then cut it out. Glue a stick onto the back of the mask so that it can be used as a fan.

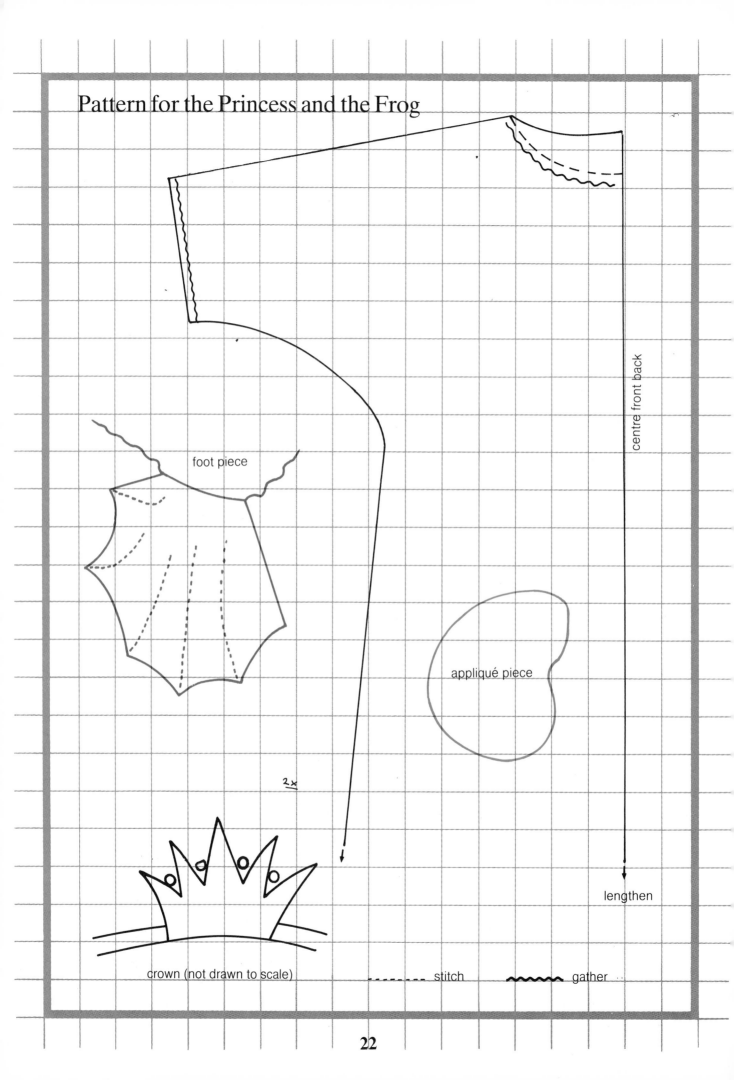

Pattern for the Princess and the Frog

centre front back

foot piece

appliqué piece

2x

lengthen

crown (not drawn to scale)   - - - - - - stitch   ∿∿∿∿ gather

22

The Princess and the Frog

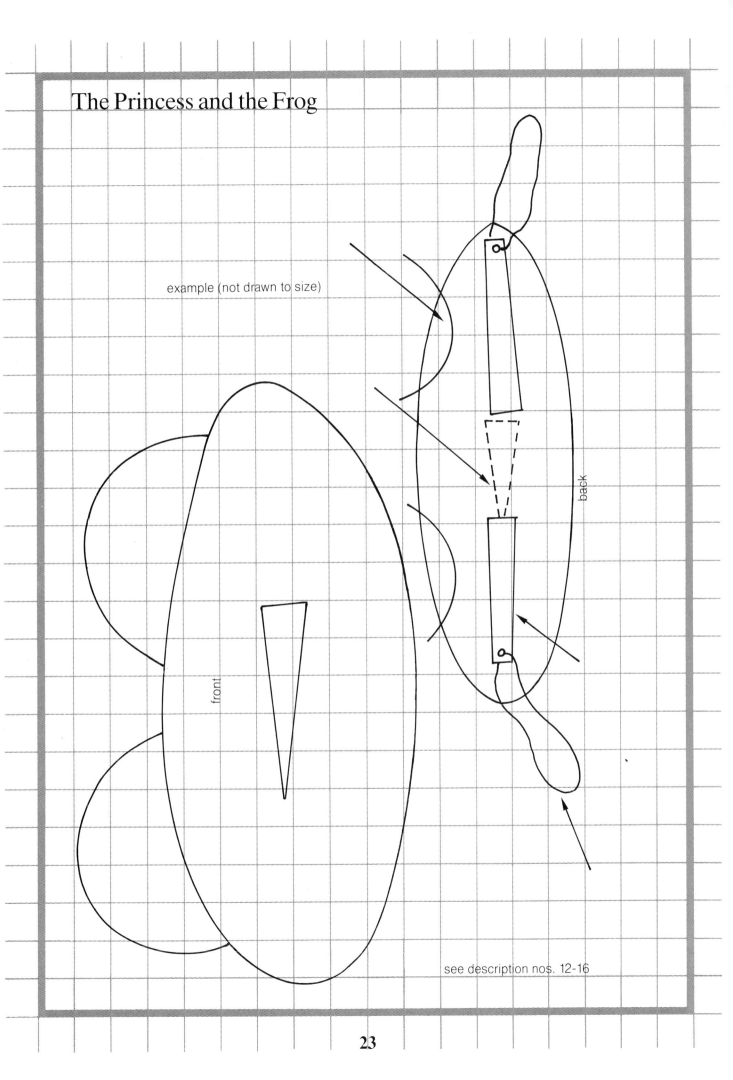

example (not drawn to size)

front

back

see description nos. 12-16

The Little Match Girl

Material for the dress and hair band
any material, 150 x 120 cm (75 x 60″)
white cotton for appliqué piece, 40 x 120 cm (20 x 60″)

In addition
red fabric dye
1 brightly coloured headscarf
1 box of long matchsticks
fabric adhesive
elastic
fibre fill 40 x 120 cm (20 x 60″)
bias binding

◄1►
Cut out the *dress*.
◄2►
Sew up shoulder seams, the centre back seam and the side seams.
◄3►
Hem around the neck edge and sleeves, and pass elastic through.
◄4►
Cut out appliqué piece for the whole width of the bottom from the white material.
◄5►
Cut out the same quantity of fibre fill.
◄6►
Place the fibre fill on the inside of the dress and the appliqué piece on the outside.
◄7►
Pin or tack the material together.
◄8►
With a pencil, draw the outlines of the matchsticks and stitch down.
◄9►
Stitch round the outline at the top with a small zig-zag stitch.
◄10►
Colour the heads of the matchsticks red with fabric dye.

◄11►
Allow the paint to dry completely.
◄12►
Finish off the bottom of the dress with bias binding or leave the frayed edges.
◄13►
To make the *hair band*, stitch together two strips of remnants of material, making them the same lenght as the circumference of the head.
◄14►
Stick the matches close together onto the strip of material, using fabric adhesive.
◄15►
Finish off the strip with a piece of elastic.
◄16►
Wear the *headscarf* round the head peasant style, i.e., with the knot on the inside.
◄17►
Fold the hair band onto the border of the forehead and wear the scarf round the head.
◄18►
The costume is finished off with gloves with rather long fingers.

Accessories
old shoes or boots

Make-up for the Little Match Girl

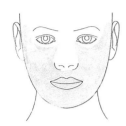   

1 Use a dermatograph pencil to make a dividing line. Silver coloured water-based make-up is applied with a small wide brush.

2 Dark blue water-based make-up is applied with a small wide brush to merge into the silver make-up.

3 The lines of the matches are indicated with a brush and some white water-based make-up.

4 Use a thin brush to fill in the matches inside the lines with white water-based make-up. Use red water-based make-up to draw in the match heads.

Useful tip
Make a simple bag from red material and fill up with home-made giant matches. These matches can be made from pieces of dowelling. The matches stick out above the edge of the bag.

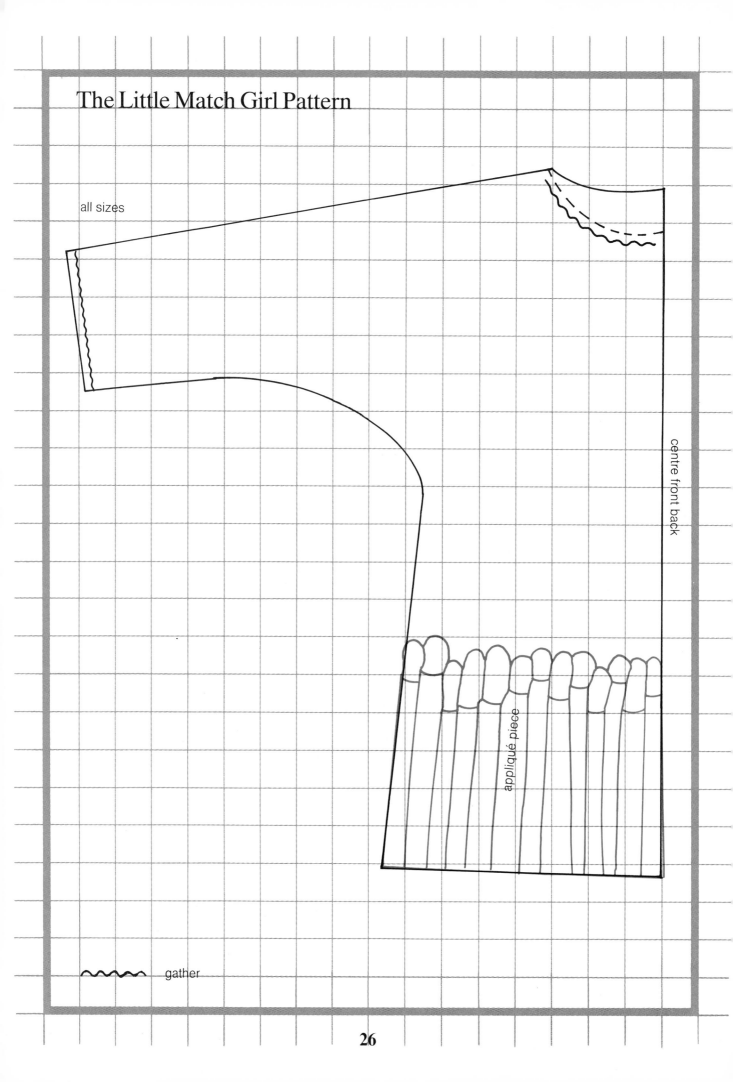

The Little Match Girl Pattern

all sizes

centre front back

appliqué piece

〜〜〜 gather

26

The Little Match Girl

example (not drawn to scale)

headscarf

scarf

head band

The Princess and the Pea

Material for the dress
any material, 150 x 120 cm (75 x 60″)
white cotton, 50 x 120 cm (25 x 60″9
white lace, narrow strip 150 cm (75″) long

Material for the petticoat
any material, 70 x 120 cm (36 x 60″)

Material for the nightcap
any material, 50 x 50 cm (25 x 25″)

◄1►
To make sure, measure the length of the child right down to his feet.

◄2►
Cut out the *dress*, and then sew up the shoulder seams, side seams and the centre back seam.

◄3►
Finish off neck edge with a narrow hem and thread the elastic through.

◄4►
Check the length of the dress, and hem.

◄5►
Thread elastic through the sleeves.

◄6►
Cut out the *skirt* 2 x from the foam plastic and then 2 x from the material, with a generous border.

◄7►
Smooth the material over the foam plastic.

◄8►
Cut wide wavy strips from the remnants of material and place these overlapping crossways over the two parts of the skirt.

◄9►
Pin down all the strips.

◄10►
Stitch the strips of material down along the dividing lines with a small zig-zag stitch.

◄11►
Now pull the edges taut.

◄12►
Using a slightly larger zig-zag stitch, sew along the whole outline of the parts of the skirt over the edge of the foam plastic.

◄13►
Finish off with bias binding.

◄14►
Fold the bias binding and sew down as a narrow border.

◄15►
On both sides of the parts of the skirt, sew pieces of tape about 20 cm (10″) apart. These can be tied in a knot to fasten over the skirt.

◄16►
Hem a strip of white cotton 20 (10″) wide and the length

In addition
various pieces of any coloured material
bias binding 300 cm (150″)
elastic
Velcro 30 cm (15″)
thin foam plastic or fibre fill 70 x 120 cm (35 x 60″)
a ping-pong ball painted brown, green or gold
a piece of thick gold paper or card
of the waist, and on one side sew on a piece of lace.

◄17►
Sew the other side on to the top of one of the pieces of the skirt and fold the material over the patchwork skirt like a sheet.

◄18►
Attach the ping-pong ball almost at the bottom of the skirt using strong thread and a large needle.

◄19►
Cut the *top of the skirt* 1 x from foam plastic and 1 x from the white material.

◄20►
Sew up the side and the long top.

◄21►
Turn the bag inside out and slide the foam plastic in.

◄22►
Sew up the bottom.

◄23►
Stick the cushion down on all sides about 3 cm (1.5″) from the edge.

◄24►
Sew on a piece of lace at the top.

◄15►
Sew the bottom of the cushion onto the top of the other part of the skirt.

◄26►
Sew a piece of Velcro onto the inside of the cushion by hand and then do this again at the same height on the back of the dress so that the cushion and the dress can be stuck together.

◄27►
Cut a circle from the material for the nightcap (diameter about 50 cm (25″)).

◄28►
If required, sew on a piece of lace.

◄29►
Sew a narrow tunnel about 6 cm (3″) from the edge and thread elastic through so that it can be pulled to the required size.

◄30►
Cut a small crown from gold paper or card and fix onto the front of the nightgown.

Accessories
tights, shoes and gloves

Make-up for the Princess and the Pea

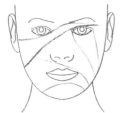

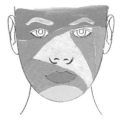

1 Use a dermatograph pencil to lightly draw lines on the face.

2 Colour in the spaces with red, purple, orange, green, silver, gold and yellow water-based make-up.

3 Emphasize the eyebrows using silver coloured water-based make-up.

4 Colour the lips bright red.

Useful tips
A Princess wears lace gloves and rich jewellery. It is appropriate to varnish the nails gold or silver.

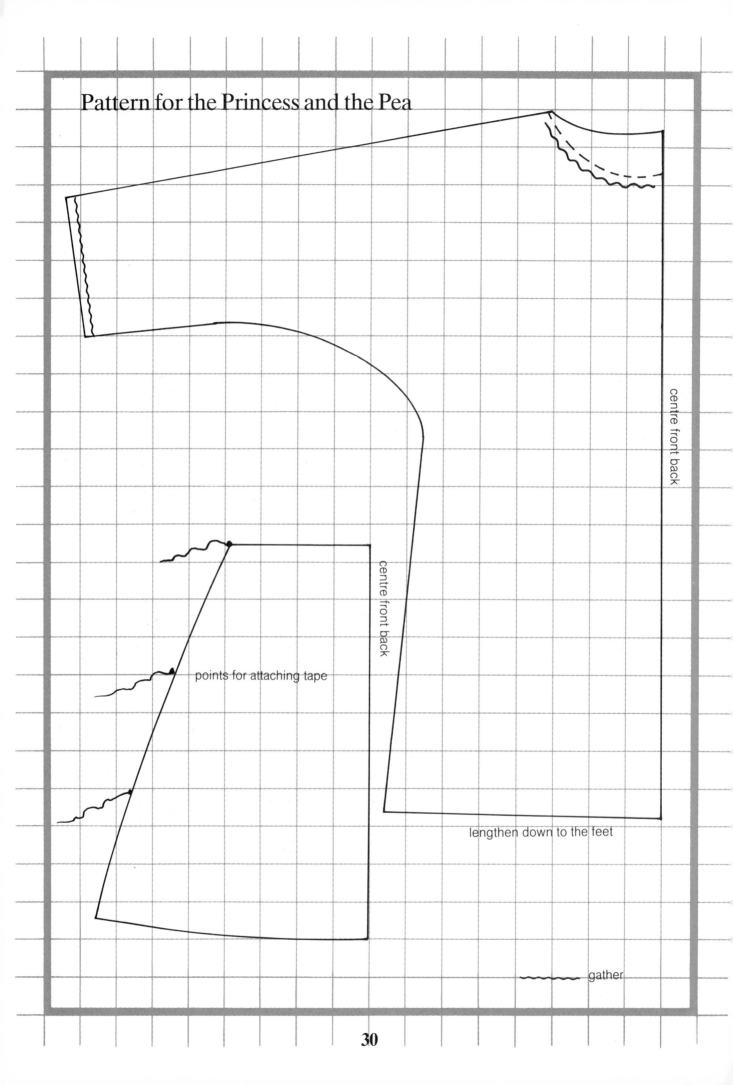

Pattern for the Princess and the Pea

centre front back

centre front back

points for attaching tape

lengthen down to the feet

〜〜〜 gather

The Princess and the Pea

example (not drawn to scale)

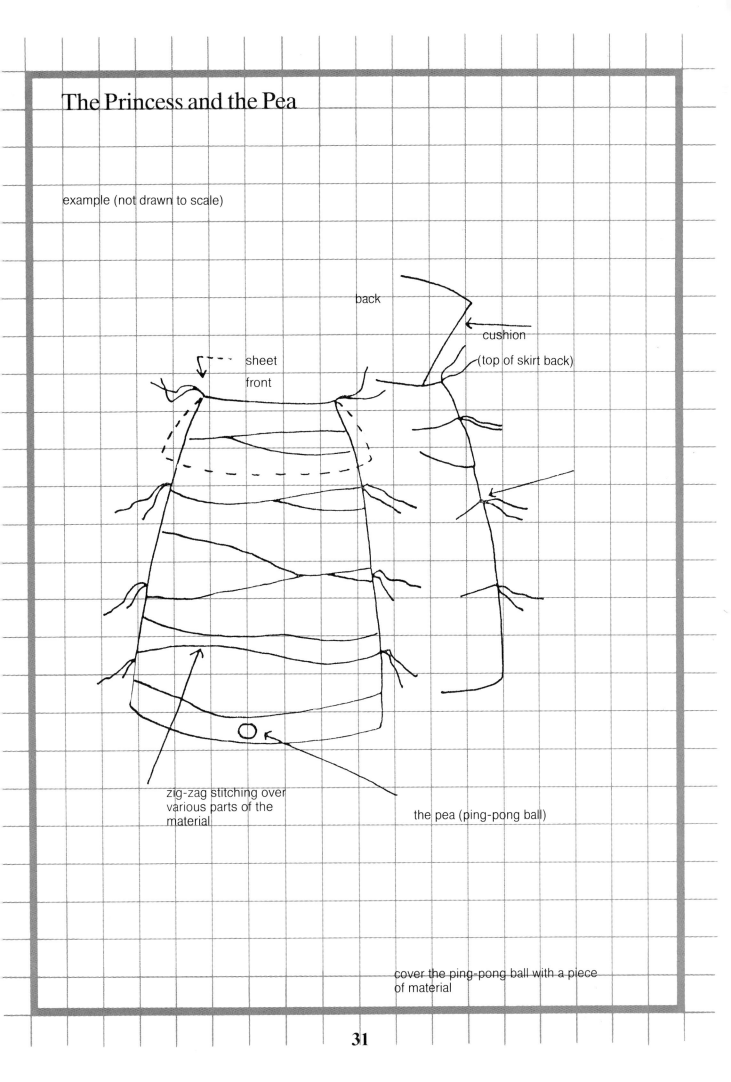

back

cushion

(top of skirt back)

sheet

front

zig-zag stitching over
various parts of the
material

the pea (ping-pong ball)

cover the ping-pong ball with a piece
of material

Ali Baba

Material for the trousers
any material, 80 x 120 cm (40 x 60")

Material for the shirt
any material, 50 x 120 cm (25 x 60")

Material for sash and turban
any material, 100 x 120 cm (50 x 60")

In addition
foam plastic or fibre fill, 30 x 120 cm (15 x 60")

◀1▶
Cut out the trousers.
◀2▶
Sew up seams centre front and centre back.
◀3▶
Cut out a strip the same length as the top of the trousers from the foam plastic or fibre fill.
◀4▶
Sew up inside seams and outside seams.
◀5▶
Sew the foam plastic or fibre fill about 3 cm (1.5") from the top of the trousers onto the inside. Hem the waistband and thread elastic through.
◀6▶
Hem trouser legs and pass elastic through.
◀7▶
Cut out the *shirt.*
◀8▶
Sew up centre front and centre back to the indicated point.
◀9▶
Hem the neck edge and fasten the centre back with hooks and eyes.

◀10▶
Hem the sleeves and pass elastic through.
◀11▶
For the *collar.*
cut a strip about 12 cm (6") wide and the length of the circumference of the neck from a remnant of foam plastic or fibre fill.
◀12▶
Cover the foam plastic or fibre fill with the material for the collar.
◀13▶
Fasten centre back with hooks and eyes.
◀14▶
Divide the rest of the material into two long strips. Hem these, and wind one round the head as a turban and the other round the waist as a sash.

Accessories
earring
mules

Make-up for Ali Baba

  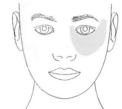 

1 Use a natural make-up to cover the face thinly and evenly.

2 Powder the face lightly and then use a brush to draw in a yellow shape under the eye with water-based make-up.

3 Use a black and a brown dermatograph pencil to draw in the eyebrows.

4 Draw a small black moustache just under the nose with a small hard brush and water-based make-up. The lips are made up in an orange red colour.

Useful tips
Stick a few toy daggers in the sash. The image is enhanced with some rattling chains and a large cable.

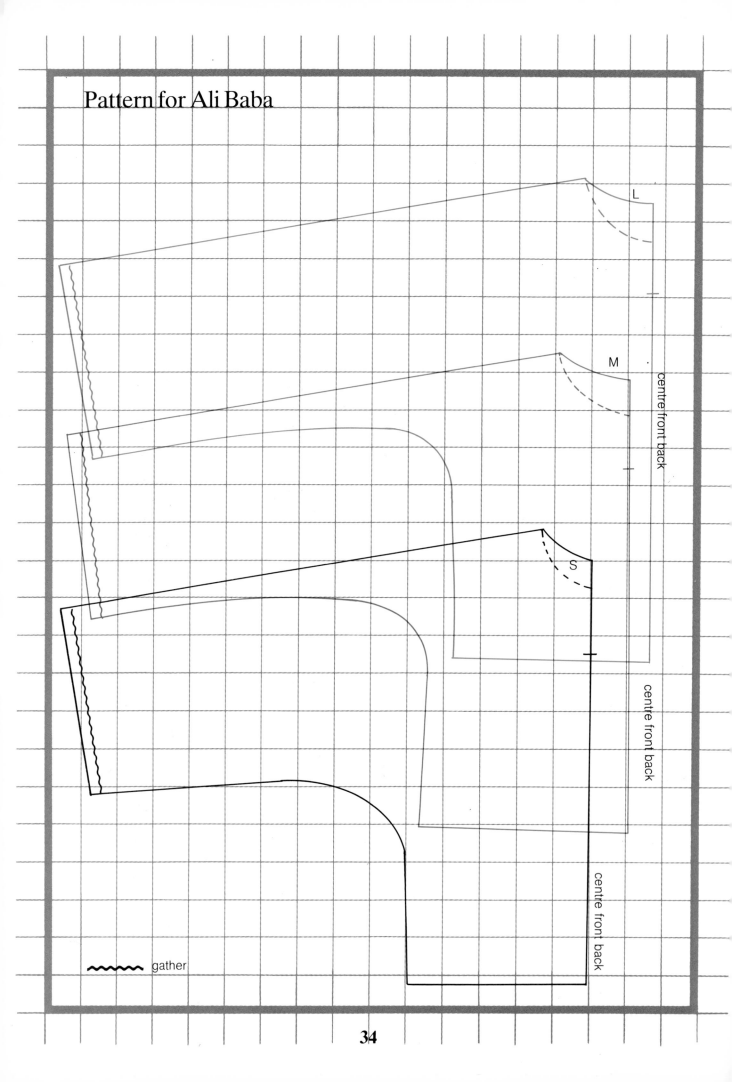

Pattern for Ali Baba

L

M

S

centre front back

centre front back

centre front back

~~~~~ gather

34

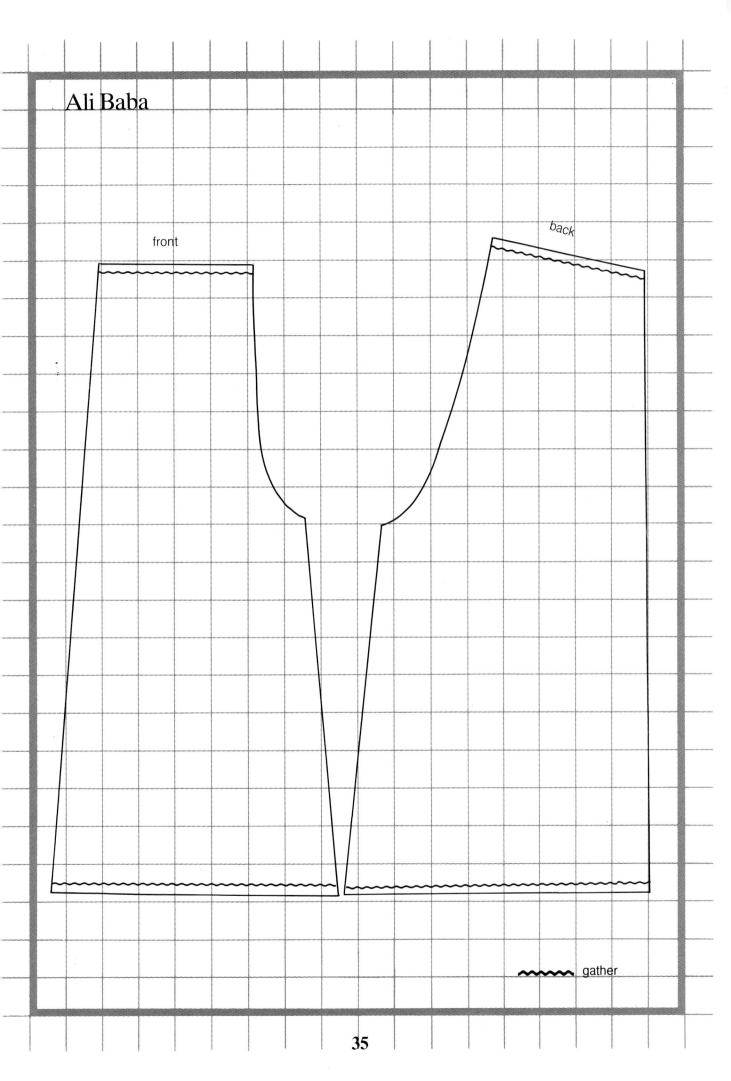

Ali Baba

front

back

gather

The Golden Goose

Material for trousers
any material, 80 x 120 cm (40 x 60")

Material for the shirt
any material, 50 x 120 cm (25 x 60")

Material for the goose
any white material, 40 x 120 cm (20 x 60")
orange material, 30 x 120 cm (15 x 60")
gold coloured material, 30 x 30 cm (15 x 15")

In addition
Thin foam plastic 40 x 120 cm (20 x 60")
elastic
hooks and eyes

◀1▶
Cut out the *trousers*.
◀2▶
Sew up centre front and centre back up to the indicated points.
◀3▶
Sew up the inside leg seam and the outside leg seam.
◀4▶
Finish off the top and bottom with a small hem and pass elastic through.
◀5▶
Cut out the *shirt*.
◀6▶
Sew up centre back seam up to the indicated point.
◀7▶
Fasten sleeves and side seams.
◀8▶
Finish off sleeves with a hem and pass elastic through.
◀9▶
Finish off neck edge with a hem and fasten centre back with hooks and eyes.
◀10▶
Cut two triangles from the bottom and finish off with a zig-zag stitch.
◀11▶
Loosely tie a belt round the waist.
◀12▶
Cut a strip 40 x 60 cm (20 x 30") from the orange material.
◀13▶
Hem the short sides, sew the long sides together and turn the material inside out.
◀14▶
Fold the material along the length and stitch two tubes down the entire length.
◀15▶
Thread elastic through and pull tight so that it fits around the neck.
◀16▶
Cut out the *goose* 2 x from the foam plastic.
◀17▶
Also cut out *goose* 2 x from the white material.

◀18▶
Lay the white material onto the foam plastic and smooth out.
◀19▶
Lay the two pieces with the right sides together.
◀20▶
Sew the two parts together, except for the bottom of the belly.
◀21▶
Turn the goose inside out.
◀22▶
Cut the *webbed feet* and *beak* from the foam plastic 2 x.
◀23▶
Cover these on both sides with orange material by hand.
◀24▶
Sew up the bottom of the belly by hand, sewing in the webbed feet.
◀25▶
Sew the two parts of the beak onto the head so that the thick part of the beak falls slightly over the cheek.
◀26▶
Cut the wings from the golden material and sew loosely onto the body.
◀27▶
Cut the other webbed feet (for the feet) 2 x from the foam plastic.
◀28▶
Cut out from the orange material leaving a generous border.
◀29▶
Lay the material on the foam plastic and stitch the edges with a small zig-zag stitch.
◀30▶
Cut away excess material, sew in pattern seams.
◀31▶
Sew elastic onto the ends so that the webbed feet can be worn round the ankles, just above the shoes.

Accessories
shoes
belt or tape of gold coloured material

Make-up for the Golden Goose

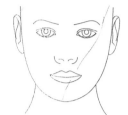 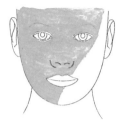  

1 Use a black dermatograph pencil to draw a line on the face.

2 Apply a gold coloured water-based make-up to the right half of the face with a small white brush and white water-based make-up to the left half of the face.

3 The feathery effect is obtained by applying white make-up several times with a brush.

4 The eyebrows are made up using the colour of the belt or sash. The lips are made up red.

Useful tip
Make a hat of gold material or card. Measure the circumference of the child's head. Cut out two halves of the head (see illustration) and stitch together, folding the bottom of the hat in or out.

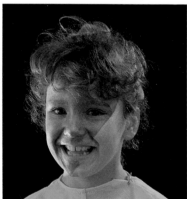

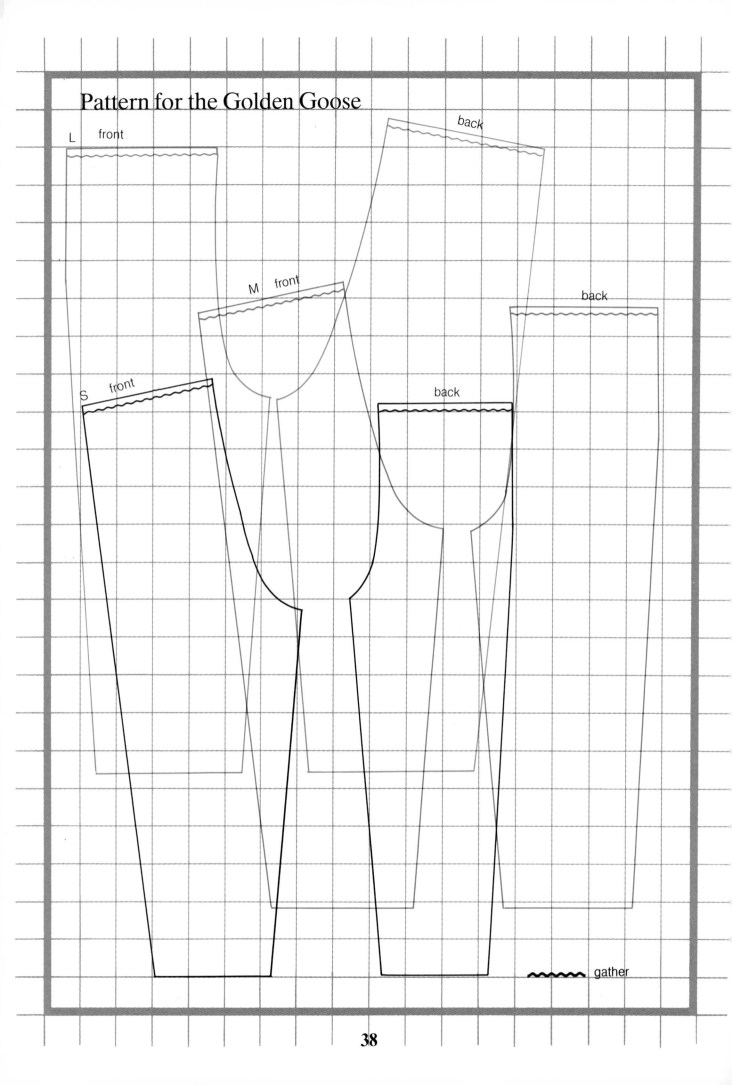

Pattern for the Golden Goose

L front

back

M front

back

S front

back

gather

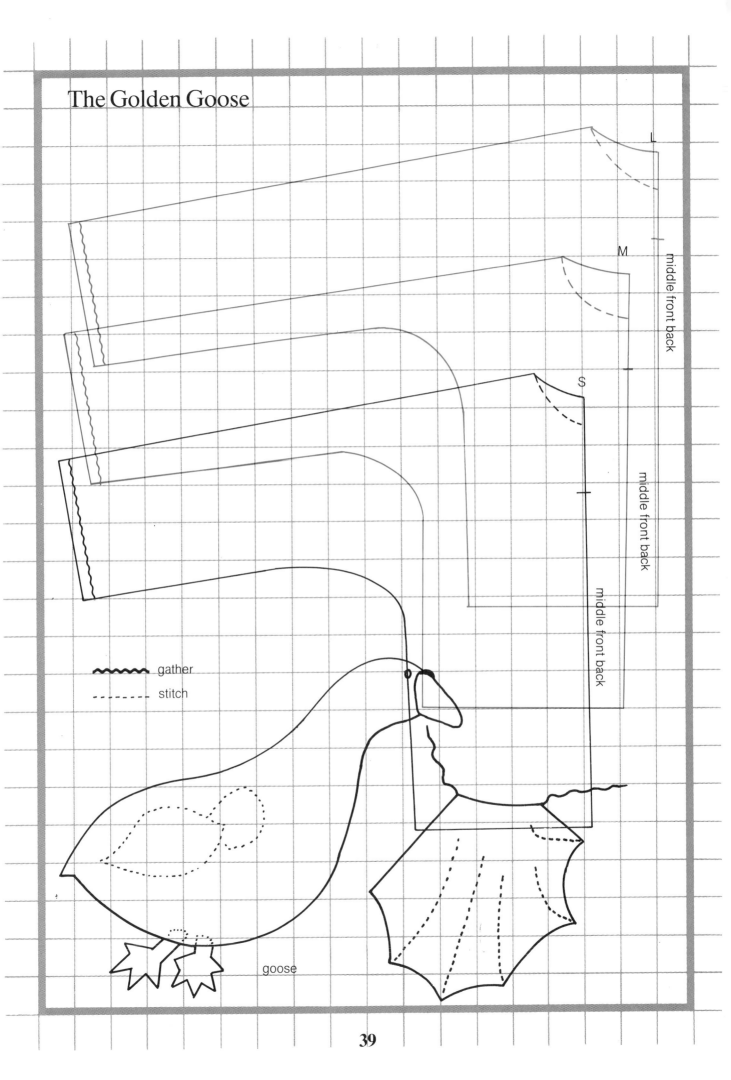

The Golden Goose

gather
stitch

middle front back

middle front back

middle front back

L
M
S

goose

39

The Sorcerer's Apprentice

Material for the trousers
any material, 70 x 120 cm (35 x 60")

Material for the shirt
any material, 50 x 120 cm (25 x 75")

Material for the cape
any material, 120 x 120 cm (60 x 60")

Material for the hat
felt card, 40 x 80 cm (20 x 40 cm")
or card with material glued onto it

◄1►
Cut out the *trousers*.
◄2►
Sew up the outside leg seams and the inside leg seams,
and then the centre front and centre back seams.
◄3►
Hem trouser legs and waist and pass elastic through.
◄4►
Cut out the *shirt*.
◄5►
Sew up centre completely and centre back up to the indicated point.
◄6►
Hem neck edge and fasten centre back with hooks and
eyes.
◄7►
Hem sleeves and pass elastic through.
◄8►
Hem a wide strip of the remaining material and use this
as a belt.
◄9►
Fold the material for the *cloak* and cut one layer open
halfway down the centre. See illustration on p. 43.
◄10►
Hem the edges.
◄11►
Place the cloak over the child's shoulders so that the
arms are held out to the sides. The material should fall
just over the child's hands. Then hem round the material. If required, sew up some of the side seams or other-
wise tie them up with tape.
◄12►
The remaining material can be used to cover the *hat*.

In addition
gold stars or other decorations
two sheets of silvery or other shiny card
elastic
Velcro 40 cm (20")
hooks and eyes

◄13►
Cut the circle with a diameter of about 40 cm (20") from
the card for the hat. Cut the circumference of the child's
head from this circle.
◄14►
Fold a pointed cone from the remaining card with a diameter slightly larger than that of the rim that has al-
ready been cut out.
◄15►
Glue the side of the pointed cone down at the required
size.
◄16►
Slide the cone as far as possible into the rim and make
cuts round the edge of the cone. Fold the flaps round
and glue them onto the rim. It is possible to finish off the
top with a thin strip of material.
◄17►
The *wig* is made from cotton threads cut to the right
length and stitched onto a strip of material. This strip of
material should be about three quarters of the length of
the opening of the hat.
◄18►
Sew a strip of Velcro onto one side of the strip of material with the hairs on it. The other half of the Velcro is
stuck into the opening of the hat.
◄19►
The top parts are joined together and can be easily sepa-
rated.

Accessoires
Chinese slippers
gloves
'magical ball' (balloon or white ball)

Make-up for the Sorcere's Apprentice

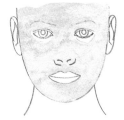

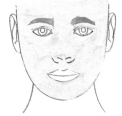

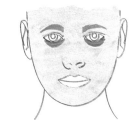

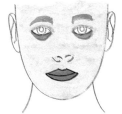

1 Apply silver coloured water-based make-up with a sponge and a small wide brush. Don't forget to apply make-up to the neck as well.

2 Colour in the eyebrows with blue water-based make-up.

3 A bluish-green water-based make-up is applied under the eyes.

4 The lips are coloured blue.

Useful tips
Attach strips of coloured gauze to the point of the hat. Also drape long strips of gauze round the neck. Make sure that the colours go together well.

Pattern for the Sorcerer's Apprentice

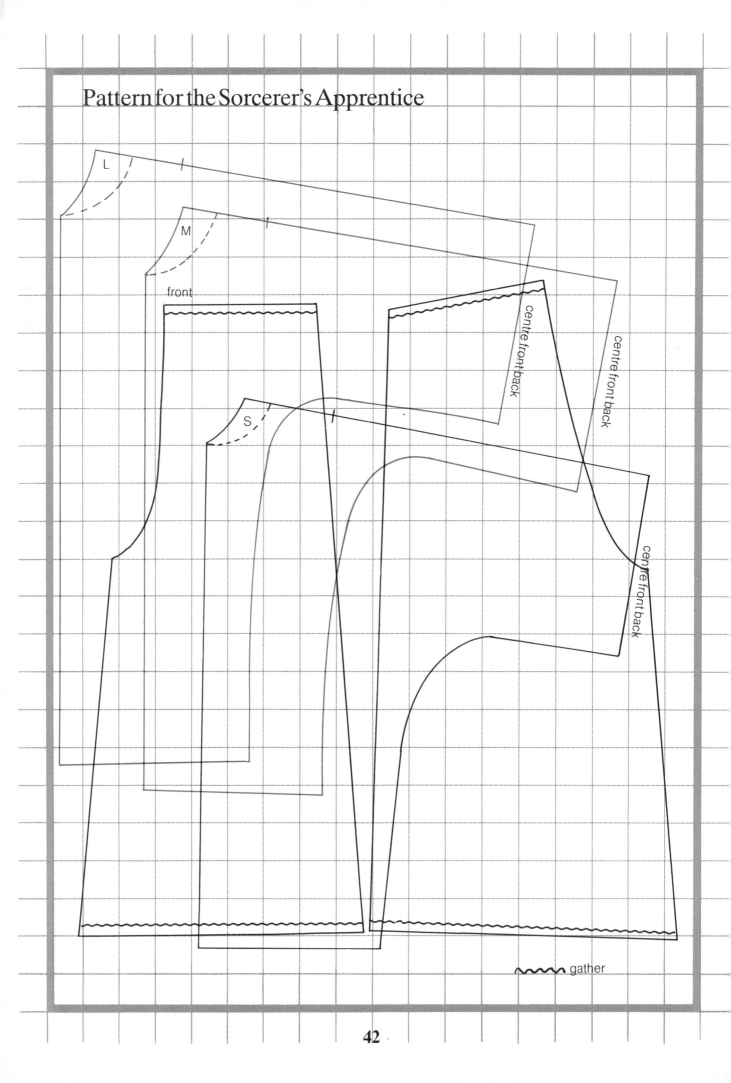

L

M

front

S

centre front back

centre front back

centre front back

~~~~~ gather

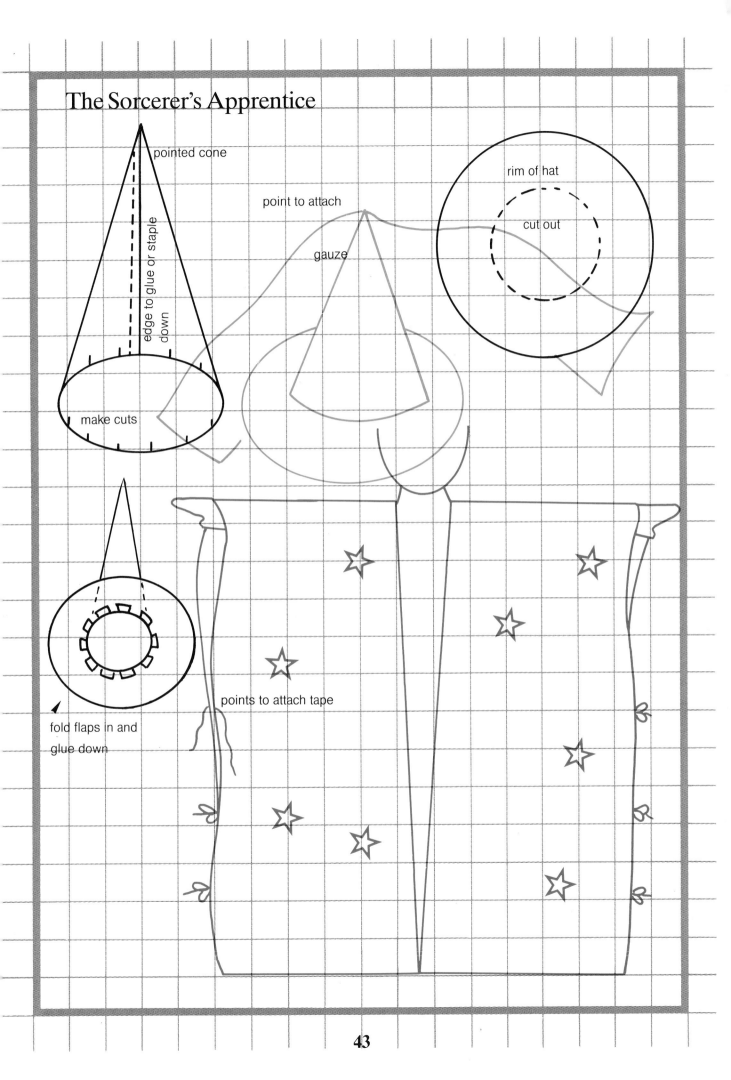

The Sorcerer's Apprentice

pointed cone

point to attach

rim of hat

cut out

gauze

edge to glue or staple down

make cuts

points to attach tape

fold flaps in and glue down

Little Red Riding Hood

Material for the dress
any material 120 x 120 cm (60 x 60")

Material for the hood and cape
any material, 80 x 120 cm (40 x 60")

In addition
a strip of fibre fill 30 x 120 cm (15 x 60")
100 cm (50") cord or rope
elastic

◄1►
Cut out the *dress.*
◄2►
Sew up centre back, shoulders and side seams.
◄3►
Place fibre fill on the inside of the material (at the bottom of the dress) and fold hem in.
◄4►
Pin the material.
◄5►
Use a pencil to draw the outline of ferns and trees.
◄6►
Stitch these pattern lines with a small zig-zag stitch.
◄7►
Finish off neck and sleeves with a small hem.
◄8►
Pass elastic through.
◄9►
Cut out cape and hem centre front.
◄10►
Sew up shoulder seams.
◄11►
Finish off the bottom with a hem.

◄12►
Cut out hood 2 x.
◄13►
Place the two parts of the hood on top of each other, right sides together.
◄14►
Sew the two parts together, except for the bottom edge.
◄15►
Sew the bottom onto the right side of the cape. Sew up the inside by hand.
◄16►
If the neck opening is too wide, sew up a tube and pass elastic through.
◄17►
Tie the cord loosely round the waist.
◄18►
Fill a basket with clearly identifiable provisions.

Accessories
tights
shoes
pin or ribbon to fasten the cape
basket

Make-up for Little Red Riding Hood

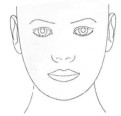  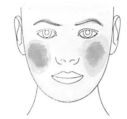 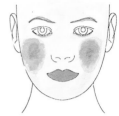

1 Light pink water-based make-up is applied with a sponge and then red make-up is used to put a blush on the cheeks.

2 The outlines of the flowers are drawn in with a dermatograph pencil.

3 Use red and yellow water-based make-up to colour in the flower patterns.

4 The lips are made up green, or any other colour that you choose.

Useful tips
To fasten the cape use a decorative brooch or large decorative ribbon.
The whole effect can be enhanced with little bunches of flowers on the shoes.

Pattern for Little Red Riding Hood

all sizes

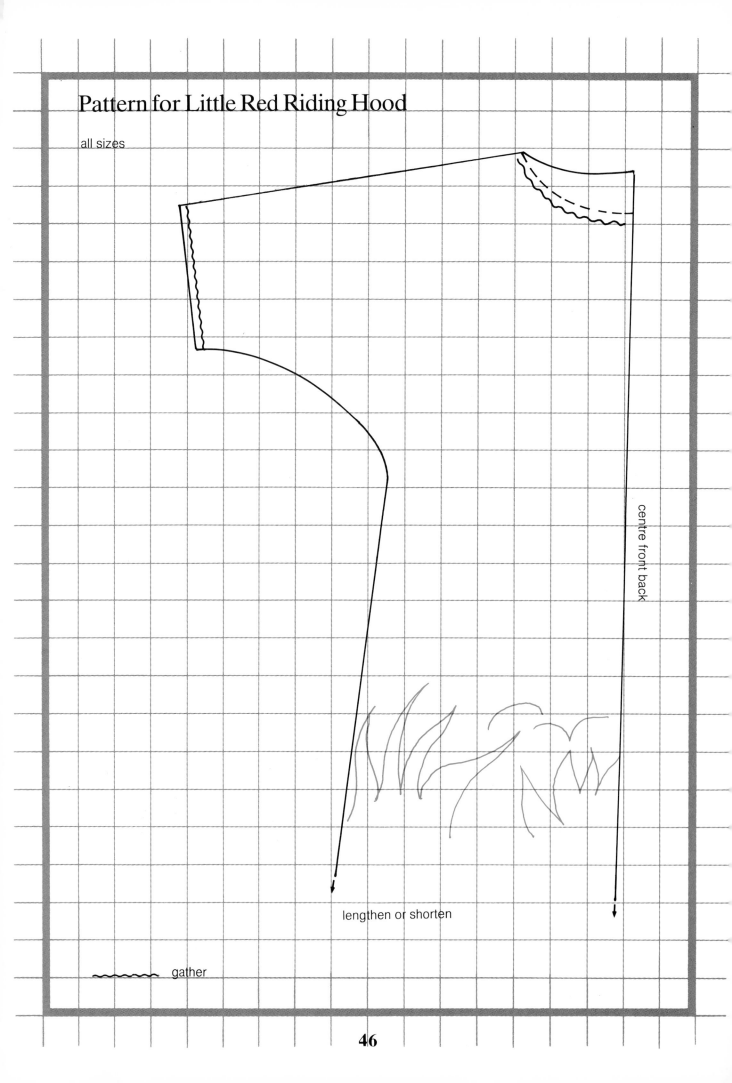

centre front back

lengthen or shorten

〜〜〜〜〜 gather

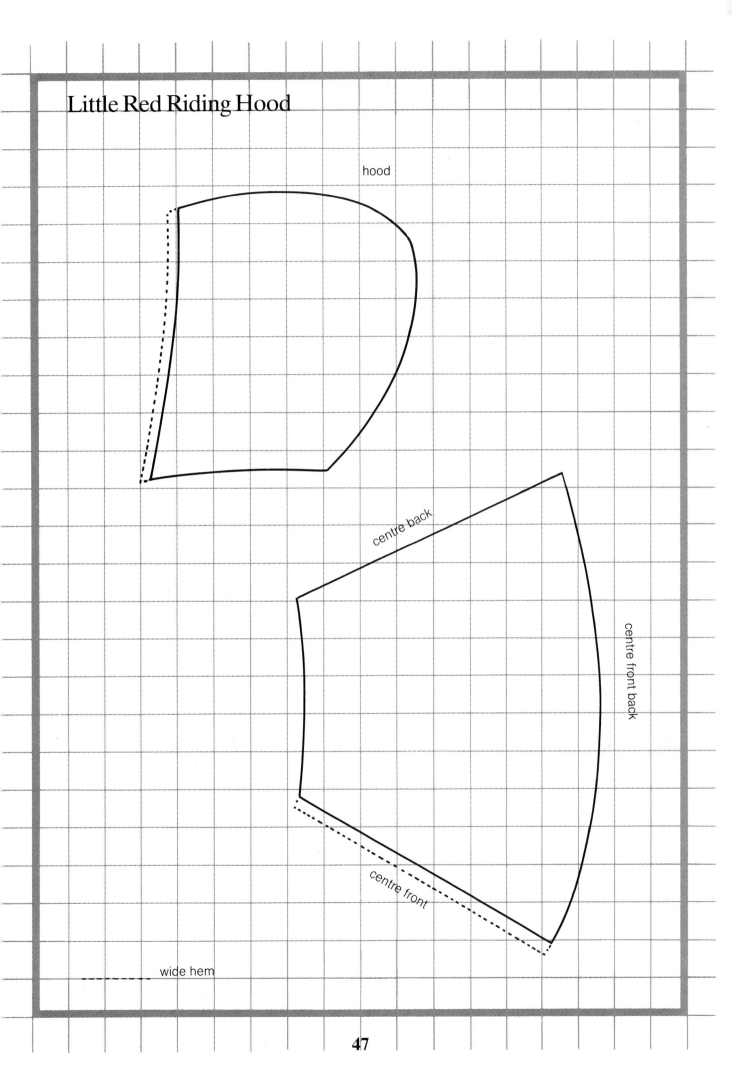

Little Red Riding Hood

hood

centre back

centre front back

centre front

wide hem

Pied Piper of Hamelin

Material for the shirt
any material, 60 x 120 cm (30 x 60″)

Material for the cape
any material, 40 x 120 cm (20 x 60″)

Material for the trousers
any material, 70 x 120 cm (35 x 60″)

Material for the hat
felt or other strong material which frays
40 x 80 cm (20 x 40″)

Material for the rats
black felt

◄1►
Cut out the *shirt.*
◄2►
Sew up shoulder seams and centre back seam up to the indicated point.
◄3►
Sew up side seams.
◄4►
Finish off neck edge with a small hem, and fasten centre back with hooks and eyes.
◄5►
Finish off sleeves with a hem and pass elastic through.
◄6►
Cut out the bottom in a wavy line and finish off the edge with a zig-zag stitch.
◄7►
Cut out the *cape* and the *collar.*
◄8►
If necessary, cut out the collar 2 x.
◄9►
If it is cut out 2x, stitch together bottom and sides of the collar and turn inside out.
◄10►
Finish off centre front of the cape with a hem.
◄11►
Sew the collar onto the inside of the cape and hem the inside by hand.
◄12►
If the neck edge is too wide, stitch a tube in the collar to pass elastic through.
◄13►
Finish off the bottom of the cape with a hem.

In addition
small black buttons
300 cm (150″) thin black cord
hooks and eyes
elastic

◄14►
Cut out about 10 *rats* from the black felt. Make tails with the thin cord and sew onto the cape here and there with small buttons (to form the eyes).
◄15►
Cut out the *trousers.*
◄16►
Sew up the inside and outside leg seams and centre back (not necessarily all the way up).
◄17►
Finish off waist with a hem and pass elastic through.
◄18►
Finish off trouser legs with a hem.
◄19►
Cut a circle with a diameter of about 40 cm (20″) from the felt for the *hat.*
◄20►
Cut out the circle from this with the circumference of the child's head (or slightly larger).
◄21►
Cut out another circle with a diameter of about 20 cm (10″) from the felt.
◄22►
Gather the edge of the first circle. This forms the crown for the rim of the hat.

Accessories
brightly coloured tights and ankle length boots or shoes
belt
recorder

Make-up for the Pied Piper

 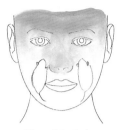  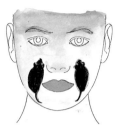

1 Apply red water-based make-up with a sponge, applying a darker colour as you go down the face.

2 Use a black dermatograph pencil to outline the rats on the face.

3 Fill in the outlines with black water-based make-up. Use grey water based make-up to draw in the rats' eyes with thin brush.

4 The lips are made up with dark red make-up. The eyebrows and eyelids are emphasized with a dark brown dermatograph pencil.

Useful hint
A recorder or flute is essential. Cut out small rats from the remaining black felt. Stitch them onto a cord. This will provide the pied piper with a long string, he can carry along.

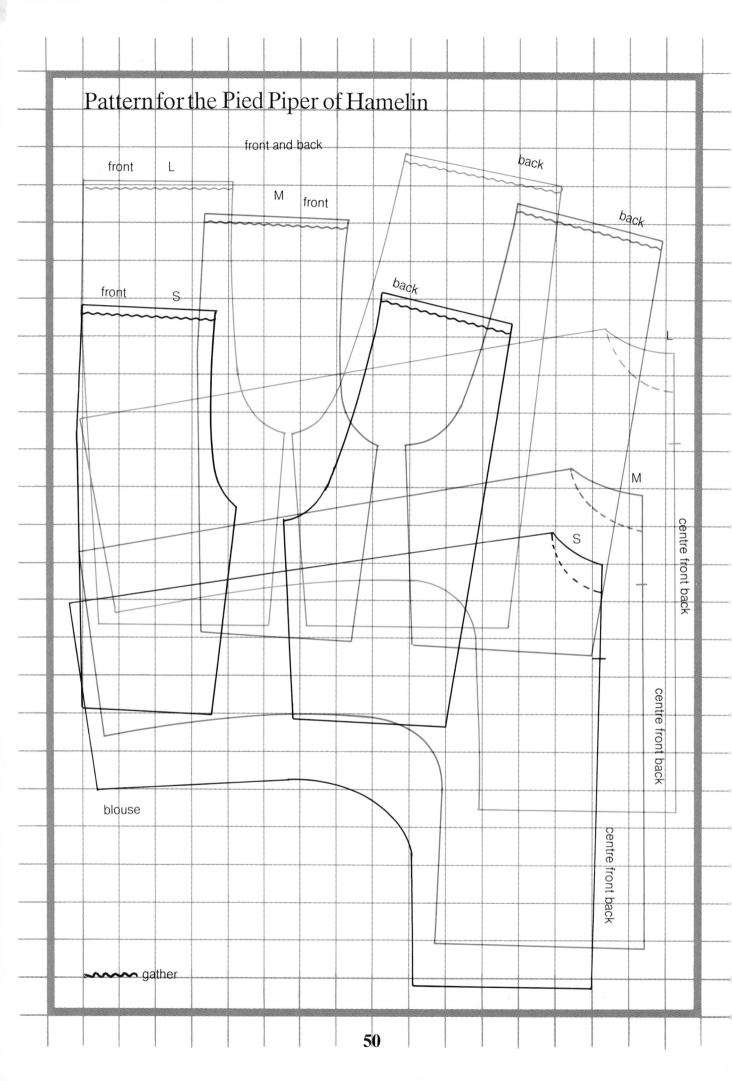

Pattern for the Pied Piper of Hamelin

front and back

front   L

M   front

back

back

front   S

back

L

M

S

centre front back

centre front back

centre front back

blouse

〜〜〜〜 gather

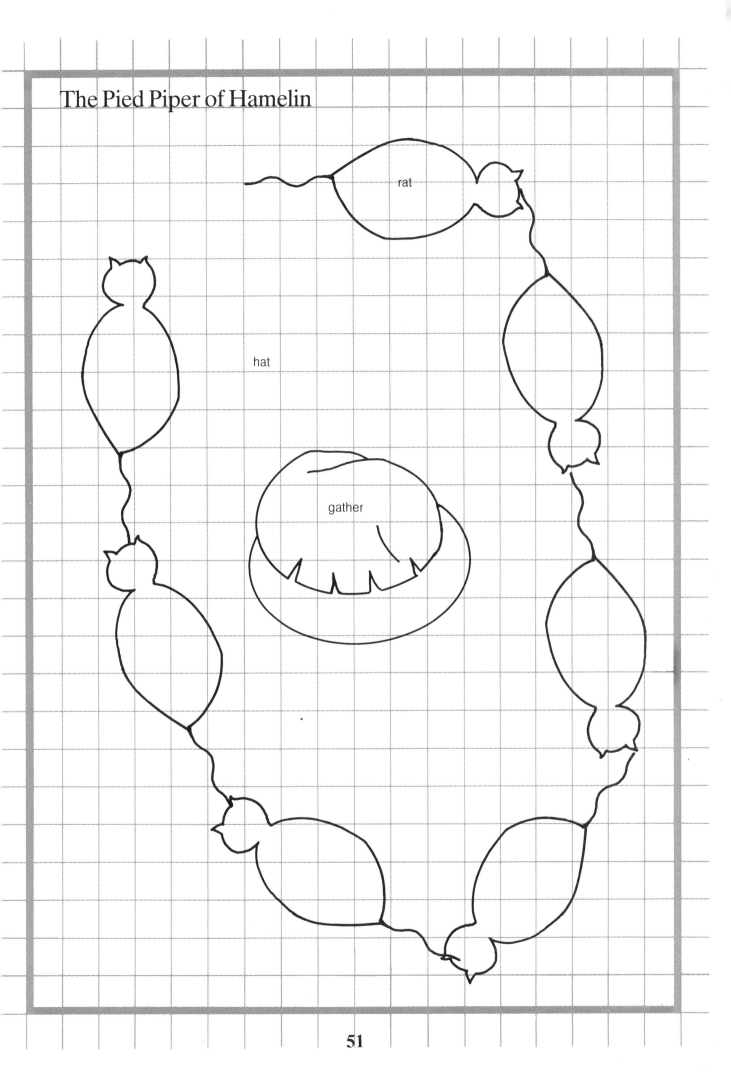

rat

hat

gather